The Dead Se

Palindromes

You may also enjoy

Put Up & Shut Up : The 90s in cartoons so far, by AISLIN & Hubie Bauch
Everything Men Know About Women, by Knott Mutch

Ask for them at your favorite bookstore

Cataloguing In Publication Data (Canada)

Richler, Howard, 1948-

The Dead Sea scroll Palindromes
ISBN 1-895854-49-0
1.   Bible - Humor.   2.   Bible - Caricatures and cartoons
I.   Shanahan, Danny.   II.   Title.

BS680.W63R52   1995   220'.0207   C95-941409-6

To receive a catalogue of our available books, please mail your request to:
Robert Davies Publishing, P.O. Box 702, Outremont, Quebec, Canada H2V 4N6,
or e-mail to http://www.rdppub@vir.com

The Dead Sea Scroll Palindromes

(edited) by

Howard Richler

Illustrated by Danny Shanahan

ROBERT DAVIES PUBLISHING

MONTREAL—TORONTO—PARIS

ISBN 1-895854-49-0

This book may be ordered in Canada from

General Distribution Services,

1-800-387-0141 / 1-800-387-0172

FAX 1-416-445-5967;

in the U.S.A., from Associated Publishers Group,

1501 County Hospital Road,

Nashville, TN 37218

dial toll-free 1-800-327-5113;

or call the publisher, toll-free throughout North America:

1-800-481-2440, FAX (514) 481-9973.

The publisher takes this opportunity to thank the Canada Council,
the Canadian Department of National Heritage and the Quebec Ministry of Culture
for their support of publishing.

Table Of Contents

OLD TESTAMENT

NEW TESTAMENT

Author's disclaimer

Many biblical scholars are expecting a bomb-shell with the recent release of previously un-published documents of the *Dead Sea Scrolls*. They will not be disappointed. I am happy to announce that while traipsing through the caves of Qumran, I unearthed a document that traces the history of the Bible in palindromic form, i.e., in words or phrases that read the same whether spelled from left-to-right or from right-to-left. Yes, there is divine purpose in the universe. I discovered my trove in the last palindromic year, 1991. There is, however, an even more shocking revelation. Not only is the document written palindromically —

IT IS WRITTEN IN ENGLISH PALINDROMES!!!!

We should not be totally surprised by this revelation, for there are indications of the favored status of English. It has become the lingua franca for a reason. Just as the Jews were the Chosen People, English has become the Chosen Language, supplanting Hebrew and Aramaic as the divine language.

The facts speak for themselves. Examine the biblical names **Eve**, **Hannah**, **Asa**, **Gog**, **Anna**, **Ada**m , O**nan**, **Aha**b, **Ahaz**, **Annas** and O**ded**. All these names are either palindromes or near palindromes! Was not Joshua the son of **Nun**? Was not David the son of **Jesse**? Was not **Janna** the great great great great grandfather of Jesus? Was not **Ara**m the great great great great grandson of Abraham?

Was not Jesus **deified**? Is not God referred to, in Mark 14:36, Rom.8:15 and Gal.4:6, as **Abba**? Are not both <u>Mom</u> and <u>Dad</u> palindromes? Is not the bread made for the Jewish Sabbath called **hallah**? What led to the secession of the northern tribes after King Solomon's death? It was the practice of forced labor called **missîm.**

Yes in**deed**, the Lord does work in mysterious ways. It is not mere coincidence that <u>God</u> spelled backwards is <u>dog</u> anymore than <u>evil</u> backwards is <u>live</u> or <u>Devil</u> backwards is <u>lived</u>. The Almighty does indeed have a divine sense of humor and if She (He) will allow me a palindromic pun at His (Her) expense, we are blessed in having a **droll Lord**. I have a sneaking suspicion that the universe was created to help God deal with the monotony of eternity.

Scholars were at first puzzled by the Hebrew inscription which read as follows: עברא אדמה אברהם

The enigma was solved when it became apparent that the English transliteration **Abraham Adamah Arba** was a palindrome. Numerically speaking, the inscription expresses a series of "firsts." **Abraham,** is the <u>first Jew,</u> **Adamah,** is "the ground" from whence the <u>first</u> man Adam came, and **Arba,** is the Hebrew word for the number four, the <u>first</u> squared number that doesn't reproduce itself.

I know there are Doubting Thomases out there who are saying "show us the nails". I, thus, present you with

The Dead Sea Scrolls.

Sllorcs Aes Daed Eht.

To aid those readers not well-versed in Scripture, I have included attributions of the palindromic statements.

(As fragments are being pieced together in jigsaw puzzle form on a continuous basis, this document must be seen as a "work in progress.")

OLD TESTAMENT

1) *Madam, in Eden, I'm Adam.* (Genesis 2)

In the beginning, there was Diddley-Squat. This bores God and He proclaims: "Let there be light" because it is less filling than regular, yet still tastes great. So, the Creator creates the Universe and gets a Big Bang out of his accomplishment. God divides Heaven from Earth, the "adama." And He drops the last letter in the "adama," the earth, and He creates Adam. Adam however, gets quickly bored with life in Paradise, and after developing the above inaugural pick-up line, is soon partying with everything in sight. He advises Eve, "You better move back, for I know not how big this is going to get."

2) *Reviled I did live; evil did I deliver.* (Genesis 3)

Now the Serpent is sly as a fox, and Eve is but a mere girl who has never ventured outside the Gates of Eden. Eve tells the Serpent that God has warned that if she eats from the tree in the midst of the garden she will die. The Serpent tells her not to worry because pesticides have not yet been invented. For his role in abetting this misdemeanour, God gives the Serpent a sentence of eternal sand-sucking. The Serpent feigns remorse but doesn't fool the Almighty.

3) *Mad? A gift. I fit fig, Adam.*
(Genesis 3)

Adam and Eve eat from the Tree of Knowledge. "And the eyes of them both were opened and they knew they were naked; and they sewed fig leaves together and made themselves aprons." Thus, the foundation of the schmutta business is laid.

4) *Eve damned Eden, mad Eve.*
(Genesis 3)

Adam is disconsolate as God evicts he and the Missus from Paradise. Naturally, he puts all the blame on Eve.

5) Cain, a monomaniac? (Genesis 4)

And it came to pass that Eve bears two sons. Cain is a tiller of the ground and his brother Abel is a keeper of sheep. Each of them bring gifts to the Lord in appreciation of the fine job He has done on the Garden. Cain brings the fruit of the ground as an offering and Abel gives the firstling of his flock and the fat thereof. In these early halcyon days, even God is not aware of the dangers of high cholestorol and He prefers Abel's high-fat gift. Cain is envious that God prefers Abel's catering service. So in a classic case of sibling rivalry run amok, he smites him with a rock. "And the Lord set a mark upon Cain," placing a humongous zit on his forehead.

6) *Ha! One wee ewe, Noah.*
(Genesis 6)

And it comes to pass that mankind becomes wicked. Noah and his family are virtuous but everybody else is scummed out. God tells Noah that He is going to destroy the Earth and instructs Noah to build an ark 300 cubits long, 50 cubits wide, and 30 cubits high. Noah implores God. "O Lord, can you give it to me in inches, for I don't understand the metric system."

7)   Ten animals I slam in a net.
(Genesis 7)

God tells Noah to bring along a heterosexual male and female of each species. The bees are placed in archives and the larger animals in Hippocrates. Noah's son, Ham, shows an understandable lack of delicacy in loading the snakes.

8) *Did I step on dog poop, God?*
No pets, I did!
(Genesis 7)

Noah chastizes his son Shem for trying to domesticate a Doberman.

9) Ha! On! On! On! O Noah!
(Genesis 7)

Noah's wife, *Joan of Ark,* is inspired by animal behaviour on the original love boat.

10) Was it Ararat I saw?
(Genesis 8)

On the seventeenth day of the seventh month of confinement with odiferous beasts, Noah does a double take when the ark comes to a rest upon Mount Ararat.

11) *"Pee? We bad!" Lot told Abe, "weep".*
(Genesis 13)

Lot jives his uncle Abram for having a wet dream. In Genesis 17, God changes the name to Abraham notwithstanding the Patriarch's preference for the name Melvin or for the fact that the name now has the unkosher ending "ham." As is His wont, God remains steadfast but gives Abraham title to the land of Canaan on the provision that he and his descendants cut off their foreskins and promise not to leave the tip on the table. Thus is born the first penile institution.

12) *Did I do, O God, did I as I said I'd do? Good I did!* (Genesis 18)

God wants to destroy Sodom because the natives are Sodomites. Abraham askes God if he would destroy Paris because the denizens are Parisites; Crete because they're Cretins and Lesbos for obvious reasons. God is not moved and nukes Sodom.

13) *Egad Lot, I hit old age.* (Genesis 19)

In escaping Sodom, Lot's wife looks back at the carnage and turns into a pillar of salt. As a result, she gets acute hypertension which ages her thirty years in a nanosecond.

14) *Pa's a sap!* (Genesis 19)

Lot is living in an isolated cave with his two daughters. The girls want to "preserve seed of our father," so the eldest daughter convinces her sister that if they get Dad piss drunk he won't realize what he's doing. The plan works as the girls bear sons who become the fathers of the Moabites and Ammonites.

15) *Harass selfless Sarah?* (Genesis 21)

"And Sarah saw the son of Hagar the Egyptian, which she had born unto Abraham, mocking." So Sarah gives Abraham an ultimatum; "It's me or the handmaid." Abraham chooses Sarah and extradites Hagar and Ishmael into the wilderness of Beer-sheba.

16) Knife Izzie? Fink! (Genesis 22)

Abraham is much relieved to find out that God was only teasing him when He tells him to sacrifice his son Isaac on Mount Moriah. After extensive psychotherapy to alleviate the trauma, Isaac regains his potency and sires the fractious twins Esau and Jacob.

17)   A pet? I'm Esau, a Semite, Pa! (Genesis 27)

Hairy Esau is incredulous when his dim-eyed father Isaac mistakes him for the family sheepdog.

18)   E.T., I'm Esau, a Semite.
(Genesis 32)

During his egyptian travels, Esau's camel breaks down in the middle of the desert and he's in deep dromedary doo-doo. He buys a second-hand camel from the used camel merchant Ed Tutankhamen.

19) *War, Dan? Israel clears in a draw!* (Genesis 32)

Jacob announces to his son Dan that his wrestling match with an angel has ended in a draw and that the Angel renamed him Israel. As a result of the draw, Jacob retains his BWWF (Biblical World Wrestling Federation) belt.

20) O.J. deified Jo.
(Genesis 37)

The O.J. initials refer to 'Old Jacob'. Genesis 37:3 states: "Now Israel (Jacob) loved Joseph more than all his children, because he was the son of his old age: and he made him a coat of many colours." To coin a Canaanite metaphor, this really "got their goat" because they all had to wear hand-me-downs or buy off the rack. They, thus sold Joseph to the local white traders, the Ismaelites, who broker him to the Pharaoh's captain of the guard. Joseph gains his freedom when his predictions about the commodities market help prevent a famine.

21)   On! On! On! Onan; On! On! O no! (Genesis 38)

A self-abusing Onan is bereft upon staining the family heirloom. When Onan's Mom sees the stain she says, "When I see, my son, I'm really gonna tell that jerk off." She didn't get the chance because "the thing which he did displeased the Lord; wherefore he slew him...."

22)   Egad! No brawl, a total war bondage. (Exodus 2)

The Pharaoh places the Israelite slaves under such a heavy yoke that they felt like scrambled eggs. Angered by an Egyptian's murder of a defenseless slave, Moses "looked this way and that way, and when he saw that there was no man, he slew the Egyptian, and hid him in the sand."

23) *Dog was I ere I saw God.*
(Exodus 3)

"Draw not nigh hither: put off thy shoes from off thy feet, for the place whereon thou standest is holy ground." Moses, who automatically takes his shoes off in a Japanese restaurant, forgets to remove them in the presence of the Lord and he is thus repentant.

24) *Egad, no bondage!*
(Exodus 5)

Moses comes to the Pharaoh Ramses and declares, "O great prophylactic ruler, let my people go! Grant them exit visas." Pharaoh's heart is hardened however, from eating too many of his Jewish chef's latkes and he refuses passage.

25) *Murder! Ramses marred rum.*
(Exodus 7)

A livid Moses discovers that Pharaoh Ramses has tampered with his liquor supply and all he has left to drink is kosher wine. With God's hand, he avenges this misdeed and ten terrible plagues befall Egypt. The sixth plague is boils. It is exacerbated when the instruction to "prick the boils" is reversed and pricks get boiled. From this occurence stems the term "hot tip."

26) *Dog deifers reified god.*
(Exodus 32)

The people become concerned when Moses hasn't returned from Mount Sinai after an absence of many days. They thus confront his brother Aaron, a Reform Jew: "Let us worship other gods for we do not know what has become of Moses." Aaron speaks to his brother-in-law, Nat the Contractor, and before you can say Methuselah, the Israelites construct a mall. The people worship the idolatrous god of materialism. When Moses descends Sinai he destroys the mall by making it a teen hangout.

27) *No, in uneven union.*
(Exodus 34)

Moses negotiates with God and gets the number of commandments halved from twenty-two to only eleven. Despite pleading
from Moses, God refuses to budge on adultery. The above com-
mandment was lost until its discovery in the Palindromic Scrolls.
It commands the Israelites to avoid any uneven, or odd, couplings
— especially with sheep.

28) *Must I, Moses, omit sum?*
(Numbers 35)

Moses has a pounding migraine and he climbs Sinai to get the Tablets from God. Later, Moses is told by his accountant that he can not deduct the first Tablets which he willfully destroyed.

29) Tim, must I, Moses, omit 'Summit'? (Deuteronomy 33)

Moses' editor, Tim Leviticus, tell him that due to budgetary reasons, the treatise "Summit" must be deleted and that the proposed six Books of Moses will have to be reduced to five.

30) No, siege is on. (Joshua 6)

"And the people shouted with a great shout, that the wall fell down flat, so that the people went into the city (Jericho), every man straight before him, and they took the city."

31) *Gideon. A canoe. Dig.* (Judges 7)

God tells Gideon He will help him defeat the Midianites if Gideon can find three hundred men who can dig a canoe out of the mud without any of their knees touching the ground while singing Hava Nagila.

32) *Naomi? No! Smash Samson, I moan.* (Judges 15)

A Philistine father is embarrassed when he discover that his son beat up Samson's sister Naomi rather than challenge the Biblical lethal weapon.

33) *Semite mates reverse tame times.*
(Judges 16)

Delilah explains to her parents why she prefers the Israelite Samson over nerdy Philistine boys.

34)   Go Ma, snip, "name" he-man.
Pin, Sam, Og.
(Judges 16)

Delilah discovers the secret of Samson's strength is the hair lotion he uses which is laced with anabolic steroids. Delilah exhorts her mother to shave Samson's head while her uncle Ogden attempts to immobilize him.

35) *Did Hannah say as Hannah did?* (1 Samuel 1)

"And she (Hannah)... said, O Lord of hosts, if thou wilt indeed look on the affliction of thine handmaid... and wilt give unto thine handmaid a man child, then I will give him unto the Lord all the days of his life, and there shall be no razor come upon his head." God grants her wish and she reminds God years later that she has fulfilled her part of the bargain by not ever giving her son Samuel a haircut.

36)   Gag, Agag. (1 Samuel 15)

Agag, King of the Amelekites, pleads with Samuel. "Surely the bitterness of death is past." And Samuel says, "As thy sword hath made women childless, so shall thy mother be childless among women." And Samuel hews Agag in pieces before the Lord in Gilgal.

37) *Goliath, tail Og.* (1 Samuel 17)

The leader of the Philistines <u>asks</u> Goliath (you don't <u>order</u> someone who is three cubits and one span tall) to shadow Og who he suspects of being an Israelite double agent.

38) *Now, we won.* (1 Samuel 17)

Goliath issues this challenge unto the armies of Israel: "Choose you a man for you, and let him come down to me. If he be able to fight with me, and to kill me, then will we be your servants: but if I prevail against him, then shall ye be our servants." Only David, the shepherd boy, is not afraid. He tells King Saul, "I will fight this uncircumcized giant called Phyllis Stein." And Saul replies: "Are you meschuge? You're just a little pischer." David counters: "I have already vanquished lions and bears and fear no giant since Lawrence Taylor retired." Yet, with only a slingshot, David slays Goliath. He then decapitates him enabling him to get ahead in the world. History remembers David as the second greatest King after Gretzky. David acknowledges Gretzky's superiority in Psalm 23 when he writes;

"Yea, though I skate through the valley of the shadow of
Wayne, I will fear no New Jersey Devil:
For he is with me, his passes they comfort me,
His Stanley Cups runneth over."

39) *I did David as a diva, d-did I?* (1 Samuel 18)

A stuttering Jonathan is disturbed by his desire for David. "The soul of Jonathan was knit with the soul of David, and Jonathan loved him as his own soul." After hearing of Jonathan's death, David laments, "I am distressed for thee, my brother Jonathan: very pleasant hast thou been unto me: thy love to me was wonderful, passing the love of women."

40) *Spit not on tips.* (1 Sam 18)

David saves Saul's tuches by slaying Goliath yet Saul is still unappreciative. He's brooding because women are singing a ditty which states that David's kill rate of Phillistines exceeds Saul's by a 10-1 ratio. Saul thus devises a plan to get rid of David. He tells David that he can marry his daughter Michal but will have to provide Saul with 100 Phillistine foreskins as the price for his daughter's hand. David implores, "This is too labor-intensive, Sire. It will take at least four men to hold each Philistine down while another circumcizes him." Saul replies: You putz! You can bring me the whole pickle but don't salivate on the foreskins." His task simplified, David completes his mission with dispatch and weds Michal.

41) *Live to hang;I sign a hot evil.* (2 Samuel 18)

"And Absalom rode upon a mule , and the mule went under the thick boughs of a great oak, and his head caught hold of the oak." Joab then thrusts three arrows in the heart of the dangling rebel, Absalom.

42) *My baby!/My baby!/My baby!/M_____.*
(1 Kings 3)

Two women come to Solomon's court both claiming that a baby belongs to them. Solomon asks them "Look, the kid looks like a chicken anyways. Cut him down the middle and you'll each get a drumstick and half a breast. Can't you each be satisfied with half a baby?" The true mother replies: "I want all or nothing." The pretender says, "Yeah, you got a point, Sollie, I **D**on't **N**eed **A**ll." When Solomon heard the words 'Don't Need All', he knew no real mother would say this and thus the first **DNA** test to prove parenthood was performed.

43)   Ahab! Ahab! Ahab! Aha____.
(1 Kings 21)

Jewish girls aren't good enough for Ahab and he proceeds to marry the worthless Zidonian chippy Jezebel who worships the second-rate rain god, Baal. Jezebel harangues King Ahab for sulking because Naboth won't sell him a vineyard Ahab covets. She then conspires to have Naboth killed so Ahab can expropriate the property.

44) *Drab Asa was a bard.*
(2 Chronicles 15)

As a poet, King Asa can't hold a regal menorah to King David. Asa used to bore his Judean subjects with his lousy haiku verses.

45) *Yahweh, chew hay!* (Job 2)

It was one of those uneventful heavenly days and God and the Devil are chewing the fat. God chastizes Satan about his myriad character flaws, and Satan retorts with the lame platitude, "Nobody's perfect." God replies, "What about my servant Job?" The Prince of Darkness counters, "Take away the good things in life from Job and he'll be cursing you to Kingdom Come." "You wanna bet?" bellows Yahweh. And so a challenge is set. A series of calamities strike Job. First his livestock are killed, then his servants perish followed by the death of his children. Job takes it in stride, responding thus: "You win some, you lose some." When Job was beset with an itch in the middle of his back that he can't reach, he finally cracks and curses God. God tells Job that he has no right to complain because it's His Universe and He can do what He wants to. Job apologizes and all is forgiven.

46) *Hot, oh!* (Daniel 3)

Nebuchadnezzar builds a golden statue and he commands all the nations to worhip the graven image. The Jewish princes Hananiah, Mishael and Azaria refuse to obey this dictate because it abrogates one of the Commandments of Judaism. They were also sulking at having their nice Jewish names changed recently to Shadrach, Meshach and Abednego respectively. When Nebuchadnezzar hears about their disobedience, he's ticked off. He orders the three rebels to be thrown into a furnace set a temperature seven times hotter than usual. The Almighty protects them, however, and would not let them be cooked by the flames. Thousands of years later, God shows an indifference when the Chosen People confront genocidal furnaces.

47)   *Poor Dan is in a droop.* (Daniel 6)

Enemies of Daniel conspire to have Daniel cast in a pit of lions. Not surprisingly, Daniel is feeling a bit down over the prospect of spending the night with the big tabbies. He is saved when the lions show a distaste for Jewish food.

48) *Airy, snide wolf-murder said I as red rum flowed in Syria.*
(Jeremiah 49)

Jeremiah is one of the few prophets who shows a good track record as a prognosticator. Whereas Isaiah prophesized that Jerusalem would never be destroyed, Jeremiah correctly prophesied its destruction. In the above palindromic prediction, The Lord reveals to Jeremiah that the Syrians will be plagued one day with a bloodthirsty tyrant with a near palindromic name — Assad.

49) Delivery! Revere! Very reviled! (Ezekiel 26)

Ezekiel is one manic dude. One second he's full of utter despair and the next moment he's totally serene. Perhaps, Ezekiel delivers this obscure statement while in a catatonic state of delusionary persecution. Or perhaps, he was smoking sheep droppings.

50)   *Noon. Tacit Amos saw*
I was somatic at noon.
(Amos 9)

One of Amos' fellow students recounts how Amos would shake him out of his trance when lunch was being served at the prophets-in-training academy they were attending.

51) Set? I've nine Ninevites.
(Jonah 4)

God commands Jonah: "Arise, go to Nineveh, that great city, and cry against it; for their wickedness is come up before me." Jonah replies, "You gotta be kidding, Lordie ; those Ninevites are bad dudes; they make the citizens of Sodom seem like Boy Scouts." But God isn't kidding. Jonah hightails it to Joppa to take a ship to Tarshish in a vain attempt to hide from His Omniscience. Jonah is thrown overboard when it is discovered he is using his brother Murray's student ship pass. God then arranges for a whale to swallow Jonah where he spends the next three days alternating between praying for forgiveness and hurling his guts out from the stench. When God feels Jonah is adequately contrite, He performed the Heimlich maneuvre on the beluga and Jonah is upchucked on the shores of Nineveh. He organizes a prayer quorum of ten Jewish men after God reminds him that Jonah counts as the tenth Jew.

NEW TESTAMENT

1)   *Nosh, son?* (Matthew 3)

Joseph offers Jesus his first bagel with cream cheese at his sister's sweet sixteen.

2) *Sex at noon taxes.* (Luke 2)

"And it came to pass in those days, that there went out a decree from Caesar Augustus, that all the world should be taxed." The Romans levy a tax for engaging in midday nookie.

3)   *Mary bred a Derby ram.* (Luke 2)

To supplant Joseph's meagre carpenter's income, Mary raises thoroughbred rams. The one named Shofar goes on to win the Triple Crown of sheep racing.

4) *Ah Satan, Natasha!* (Matthew 4)

Satan fails to tempt Jesus in the wilderness with exotic Russian women.

5) *Evil I did dwell; lewd did I live.* (Luke 7)

A contrite Mary Magdalene prostrates herself in front of Jesus. And he turned to the woman and said unto Simon, "Seest thou this woman? I entered into thine house, thou gavest me no water for my feet: but she hath washed my feet with tears, and wiped them with the hairs of her head."

6) *Deified name, Herod.*
Adore He, man deified.
(Matthew 14)

John the Baptist loses his head when he denounces Herod Antipas, tetrarch of Galilee, for divorcing his wife in order to marry his niece Herodias.

7) *On! I sack casino.* (Mark 11)

Jesus urges his disciples on after he overthrows the tables of the moneychangers in the temple.

8) *Rise, sir.* (John 11)

"Then when Jesus came, he found that he (Lazarus) had lain in the grave four days already... He cried with a loud voice, Lazarus come forth. And he that was dead came forth, bound hand and foot with gravecloths."

9) Lepers, alas, repel. (Matthew 8)

"And behold, there came a leper and worshipped him, saying, Lord if thou wilt, thou canst make me clean." A leper begs Jesus to cure him because his disease is putting a damper on his social life.

10) *Moody men, I pine my doom.*
(Mark 14)

Amen, enema.

Jesus is ominous at the Last Supper after eating some indigestible Passover food. God, however, provides relief.

11) *Yawn a more Roman way.*
(Mark 15)

"And Pilate asked him, Art thou the King of the Jews? And he answering said unto him, Thou sayest it." Pilate objects to Jesus's Jewish nonchalance.

12) *Was it a rat I saw?*
(John 18)
No miss, it is Simon.

Mary Magdalene asks Peter if the fleeting figure she saw was Judas.

Peter informs her it is Judas' father Simon.

13) Revere venom? Oh <u>ecce homo,</u> never ever! (John 19)

The full unabridged statement by Pontius Pilate when he presents Christ, crowned with thorns, to his accusers.

14) Tarsus rat! (Acts 9)

Saul of Tarsus (later dubbed Paul, Acts 13), is on his way to Damascus to beat up some Christians when he is blinded by a light from heaven. The Scripture in Acts 9:5 states: "And he said, Who art thou, Lord? And the Lord said, I am Jesus whom thou persecutest: it is hard for thee to kick against the pricks."

Later on, those "pricks" want to kill Saul of Tarsus for being a turncoat.

15)   No, Rome, moron!
(Acts 28)

Paul rebukes an inattentive disciple who thought he said he was going home instead of to Rome.

16)   Egad, are we not an era midst its dim arena to newer adage?
(Romans 11)

Paul sends a letter to the Christian community of Rome to boost their morale.

17) *Live not on evil deed,*
live not on evil.
1 Corinthians 6)

"Know ye not that the unrighteous shall not inherit the kingdom of God? Be not deceived: neither fornicators, not idolaters, nor adulteriers, nor effeminate, nor abusers of themselves with mankind." Paul shows zero tolerance for kinkiness.

18) *Gnostic, a tacit song.*
(1 Timothy 6)

Paul warns against the "profane and vain babblings" of gnosticism.

19) *Egad, a base note denotes a bad age.* (Revelations 6)

Saint John the Divine predicts that the Four Horsemen of the Apocalypse, Conquest, Slaughter, Famine and Death will never be as popular as the Fab Four, John, Paul, George and Ringo.